STECK-VAUGHN STUDY SKILLS FOR ADULTS

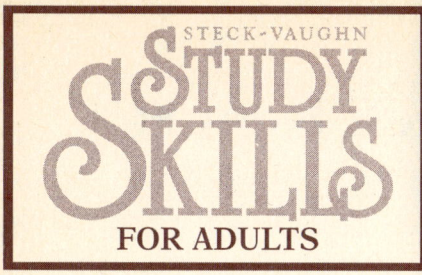

Writing Reports

Contents

LESSON 1	Preparing a Research Report		2
LESSON 2	Choosing and Narrowing a Topic		4
LESSON 3	Preparing to Do Research		6
LESSON 4	Using the Library		8
LESSON 5	Finding Information Quickly		10
LESSON 6	Taking Notes		12
LESSON 7	Developing an Outline from Notes		16
LESSON 8	Writing a First Draft		20
LESSON 9	Revising and Proofreading for a Final Report		24
LESSON 10	Preparing a Bibliography		28
REVIEW	Planning a Report		30
REVIEW	Gathering and Organizing Information		31
REVIEW	Writing a Report		32
ANSWER KEY		Inside Back Cover	

Acknowledgments

Executive Editor: Diane Sharpe
Supervising Editor: Stephanie Muller
Design Manager: Laura Cole
Cover Designer: D. Childress/Alan Klemp

Product Development: Curriculum Concepts, Inc.
Writer: Judy Rosenbaum

Illustrators: pp. 15, 26 Janet Bohn; pp. 12, 18, 24 Pam Carroll; pp. 7, 9, 16, 22 Michael McDermott; pp. 3, 11, Tom Sperling; p. 28 Lane Yerkes
Photography: cover © Tracey Borland/FPG

ISBN 0-8114-2528-2

Copyright © 1994 Steck-Vaughn Company.
All rights reserved. No part of the material protected by this copyright may be reproduced or utilized in any form or by any means, electronic or mechanical, including photocopying, recording, or by any information storage and retrieval system, without permission in writing from the copyright owner. Requests for permission to make copies of any part of the work should be mailed to: Copyright Permissions, Steck-Vaughn Company, P.O. Box 26015, Austin, TX 78755. Printed in the United States of America.

1 2 3 4 5 6 7 8 9 0 CCG 00 99 98 97 96 95 94

STECK-VAUGHN COMPANY
A Subsidiary of National Education Corporation

LESSON 1: Preparing a Research Report

A **research report** is based on information obtained from nonfiction books, magazines, encyclopedias, and other sources. It contains facts and details that support its main points. The process of writing a research report has several steps.

Ask Yourself

Suppose that you got an assignment to write a report about a famous woman. Underline each sentence that tells how you would find the information you need.

I would look up newspaper articles about her.

I would look her name up in an encyclopedia.

I would look in the library for a nonfiction book about her.

Did you underline all the items? If so, you probably have a good idea about where to find information for a research report.

How To

Prepare a Research Report

- Choose a nonfiction topic. Narrow it so it is not too broad.
- Decide which main ideas your report will cover by asking yourself what questions it will answer.
- Find information about your topic. Use sources such as encyclopedias, nonfiction books, magazines, and newspapers.
- Take notes on useful facts and details.
- Make an outline that gives main ideas and supporting details.
- Write a first draft. The first paragraph usually introduces the topic. The following paragraphs usually cover main ideas related to the topic. The last paragraph usually presents a conclusion.
- Reread your first draft to see that ideas are clearly arranged. Proofread for errors in spelling, capitalization, and punctuation.
- Prepare your final report.
- Write a **bibliography** that lists your sources if necessary.

Try It Out

Read the short report below. Then answer the questions that follow.

In the past, many South American countries had cowboys, too. The most famous South American cowboys were the gauchos of Argentina.

Argentina has many areas of grassy plains. This is perfect land for raising cattle. Cattle are raised on large ranches called *estancias*. This is where gauchos worked.

Gauchos were like U.S. cowboys in many ways. They herded and branded cattle. They did most of this work on horseback. People all over Argentina admired gauchos for their bravery and their adventure-filled lives.

Today, the way of life has changed on *estancias*. Only a few gauchos still follow the old ways. However, these brave riders will live on in stories and films.

1. What is the topic of this report?

2. What purpose does the first paragraph serve?

3. What main question does the third paragraph answer?

4. Give two facts that help answer this question.

5. What conclusion is made in the last paragraph?

What Have I Learned?

Suppose the writer also wanted to tell the history of the gaucho. On your own paper, tell where that information could go in the report.

3

LESSON 2
Choosing and Narrowing a Topic

When you choose a topic for a report, choose one that interests you. Then think about the length your report needs to be. If your topic is too broad for the space you have, narrow the topic.

Ask Yourself

Can you narrow topics? Arrange each set of topics below in order from the broadest to the narrowest by writing 1 beside the broadest topic, 2 beside the next-broadest topic, and 3 beside the narrowest topic.

A. _____ Theodore Roosevelt

_____ U.S. Presidents

_____ Roosevelt's Early Life

B. _____ U.S. Lakes

_____ Lake Michigan

_____ Lakes

C. _____ Games

_____ The History of Chess

_____ The History of Games

D. _____ How a Song Is Recorded

_____ Songs

_____ Music

Did you choose "Roosevelt's Early Life," "Lake Michigan," "The History of Chess," and "How a Song Is Recorded" as the narrowest topics? If so, you already have a good idea about how to narrow topics.

How To

Choose and Narrow a Topic

- Make a list of topics that interest you. Look at books in your school or class library to get ideas. From your list, choose the topic that interests you most.
- Ask yourself whether it will be too hard to find information about your topic. If you think so, choose another.
- Decide whether your topic is narrow enough to write about in the amount of space you have. If it is too broad, choose a smaller idea from the topic.

Try It Out

The flow chart below shows how a broad topic can be narrowed.

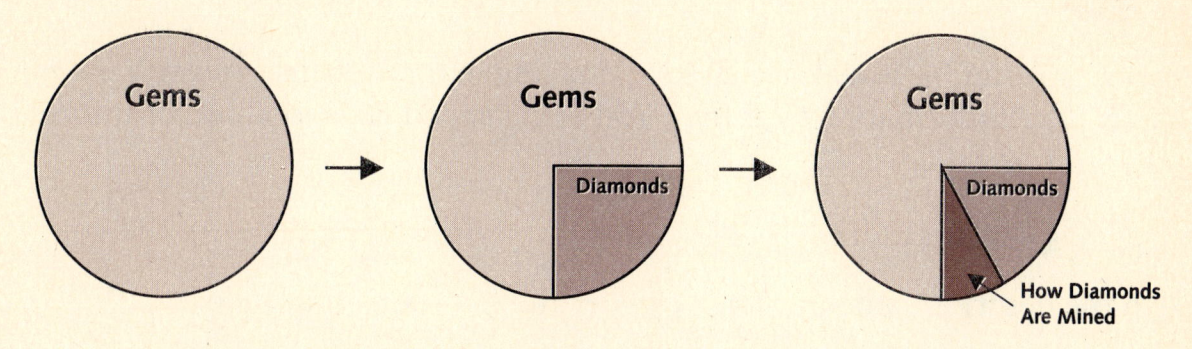

Gems → Diamonds → How Diamonds Are Mined

Using the example above, narrow each set of topics below.

1. Insects → Flying Insects → _____
2. Clothes → Shoes → _____
3. Transportation → Boats → _____
4. Weather → Storms → _____
5. Careers → Sales Jobs → _____
6. World History → U.S. History → _____
7. Literature → Poetry → _____
8. Sports → High School Sports → _____
9. Transportation → Automobiles → _____
10. Politics → Women in Politics → _____

What Have I Learned?

If you tried to write a report about a topic that was too broad, what problems might you have?

_____
_____
_____
_____

5

LESSON 3

Preparing to Do Research

Planning ahead for research will save time and effort because you will know exactly what information to gather. You won't spend time looking for information you don't need.

Ask Yourself

Read the description below. Then answer the questions that follow.

> Michael decided to write a report about Cesar Chávez, a founder of the United Farm Workers, which is a union formed for migrant farm workers. Michael immediately went to the library and gathered everything he could find about Cesar Chávez, unions, and migrant farm workers. He collected twelve books and three encyclopedias. He knew it would take hours to read them all. Yet if he only read a few, he might miss important information. With a sigh, he sat down to read all fifteen, hoping the library wouldn't close before he finished.

1. Why do you think Michael had so much trouble choosing his research books?

   _____

2. What do you think he should do before deciding which books to read?

   _____

Have you ever been in a situation like Michael's? If so, this lesson will help you plan your research wisely the next time you write a report.

How To

Prepare to Do Research

- Think about the things you already know about your topic.
- Plan the main points you will present in your report. Think of these main points as statements or as questions your report will answer. These statements or questions will help you decide what research is needed.
- To look up information about a topic, think about how the information may be organized in an encyclopedia or another source. Make a list of topic words to look up in an encyclopedia or an index.

Try It Out

For each topic below, write two questions or statements that you would choose as main ideas. Then list topic words you might use to find information. Use encyclopedias or other books for help. The first one was done for you.

1. **Topic:** The Wright Brothers and the First Airplane Flight

   Question: When did this flight take place?

   Question: How was the plane made?

   Topic words: Wright, Airplane, Flight

2. **Topic:** What Firefighters Do

   Two questions or statements: _____

   _____

   Topic words: _____

3. **Topic:** The History of My State

   Two questions or statements: _____

   _____

   Topic words: _____

4. **Topic:** How a Clock Works

   Two questions or statements: _____

   _____

   Topic words: _____

5. **Topic:** How Snowflakes Are Formed

   Two questions or statements: _____

   _____

   Topic words: _____

What Have I Learned?

Suppose you had to write a report about an inventor. On your own paper, tell why it is important to write down two questions before gathering information.

LESSON 4: Using the Library

While doing research for a report, you will probably use the library. Understanding how it is arranged can help you get the most out of its research sources.

Ask Yourself

Complete the questionnaire, based on your own experience.

1. Which encyclopedias have you used for research?

   _____

2. Place a ✓ beside the research sources you have used.

   ☐ an atlas   ☐ an almanac   ☐ a newspaper

3. If you have ever used a magazine article for research, did you find it by searching through magazines, by using the *Readers' Guide to Periodical Literature*, or by using a computer?

   _____

Have you used all the above research sources? This lesson will help you get familiar with the research sources your library has.

How To

Use Your Library

- Be organized. Use the plan you made for your report to choose sources.
- Become familiar with your library. Is there a card catalog or a computer file? Are there any reference sources on the computer? How are magazines arranged?
- Ask your librarian for help with equipment. If you avoid computers because you don't know how to use them, you might overlook useful information.
- Always use at least two sources. This makes your report more original.
- Don't rely only on encyclopedias. Other sources often give more detailed information. For example, imagine the difference between an encyclopedia article about an earthquake and an account by someone who was there.
- Be aware of copyright dates. Try to find the most current material available.

Try It Out

Do the following activity at school or at the local library. For each topic, find the suggested research sources, and write down the requested information.

1. **TOPIC:** Clipper Ships—History's Fastest Long-Distance Sailing Ships
   ENCYCLOPEDIA ARTICLE—encyclopedia's name and the article's title:
   _____
   _____

   NONFICTION BOOK—title and author:
   _____
   _____

2. **TOPIC:** The Most Recent Election for U.S. President
   ALMANAC—almanac's title and the page number:
   _____

   NEWSPAPER OR MAGAZINE ARTICLE—title of the article, the title of the newspaper or magazine, and its date:
   _____
   _____
   _____

3. **TOPIC:** Monarch Butterflies
   ENCYCLOPEDIA ARTICLE—encyclopedia's name and the article's title:
   _____
   _____

   NONFICTION BOOK—title and author:
   _____
   _____

   MAGAZINE ARTICLE—title of the article, title of the magazine, and its date:
   _____
   _____
   _____

What Have I Learned?

On your own paper, give an example of a topic you might research by looking in the following sources: newspaper, videotape of a nature program, and an atlas.

LESSON 5: Finding Information Quickly

You don't have to read an entire book or article to see if it contains what you need. You can examine it quickly by using several different techniques.

Ask Yourself

For each situation, write word-for-word if you would read every word. Write key words only if you could get needed information by doing a quick reading.

1. Your father gives you a cousin's address so you can write him a get-well card. _____

2. You get a new book. You want to see whether it contains one long story or several shorter ones. _____

3. On a shopping trip, your mother gives you a list of items that you have to find and take to the cash register. _____

4. When a school magazine comes out, you look to see how many of your friends' stories and poems are in it. _____

Did you write key words only for 2 and 4? If so, you were right.

How To

Find Information Quickly

- **Scan** material by looking for key words or words in boldface type.
- **Skim** material by reading just some sentences, especially the first or last sentences of a section, to learn what a page is mainly about.
- A library's card catalog often has a summary of the book. The summary will help you decide whether the book will be useful.
- A book's jacket, table of contents, and index will provide clues about what information the book presents.
- Charts, tables, and illustrations provide information about the book's focus.
- End-of-chapter summaries give an idea of the book's contents.
- The lead paragraph of a news article usually answers the questions who, what, when, where, why, and how. It tells what the article is mainly about.

Try It Out

In your library, find an encyclopedia, a newspaper or magazine article, and one other source that gives information about Germany. Use the reading short cuts from the **How To** box to answer the questions.

1. Which source or sources give the history of Germany in the nineteenth century?
   _____

2. Which source or sources tell about the uniting of East Germany and West Germany into the Federal Republic of Germany on October 2, 1990?
   _____

3. Which source or sources give these facts about Germany: its area, its population, and its largest cities?
   _____

4. Which source or sources give information about these German composers: Johann Sebastian Bach and Johannes Brahms?
   _____

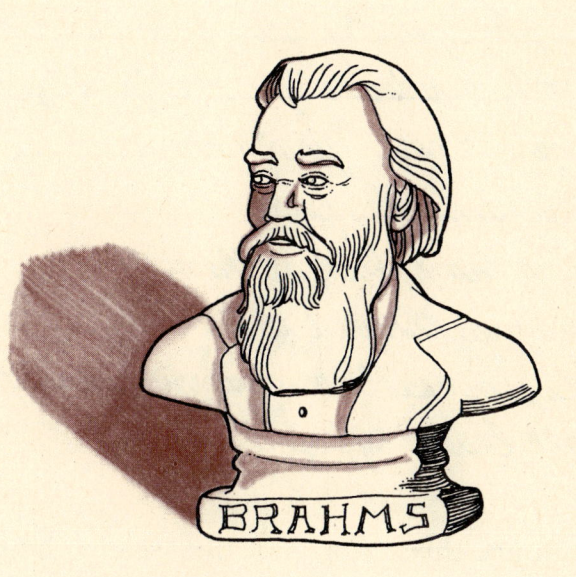

What Have I Learned?

Describe how you would quickly find information in:

an atlas _____

a magazine article _____

a nonfiction book _____

an encyclopedia _____

LESSON 6 Taking Notes

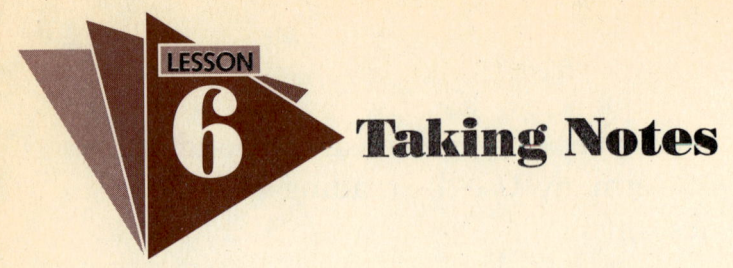

When taking notes on books or articles, make your notes serve as a first stage of writing your report. Think carefully about what you are reading before you write anything. Then, in your own words, write key words and phrases. Avoid using the exact words of an information source, but make sure your notes are accurate.

Ask Yourself

Read the information about Edward Corsi, a young Italian who moved with his family to the United States in 1907. Read the notes a student took from the information. Then answer the questions that follow.

> Two weeks after the ship set out, Edward and his family crowded at the rail of the ship in New York Harbor. They were eager to catch their first glimpse of the United States. Edward saw it first. "Mountains—look at them!" he shouted to his brother. Then they looked closer. The "mountains" were really the tall buildings of New York City.

- 2 weeks after ship set out, Edward and family crowded to rail of ship at N.Y. Harbor
- eager to catch first glimpse of U.S.
- Edward saw it first
- "Mountains—look at them!"
- Edward shouted to brother
- they looked closer—mountains really tall buildings of N.Y.C.

1. What are three words or phrases in the notes that were used as short cuts to record details? _____

2. If you were taking these notes, how would you record the information from the paragraph's first two sentences?

_____
_____

12

3. What information from this paragraph do you think might be important to write down word-for-word?

_____

4. What other short cuts for words or phrases might this student have used in taking notes?

_____

Did you know how to restate the first two sentences in your own words? If so, you are on your way to being a good notetaker.

How To

Take Notes

- Write only key words and phrases. These key words should include main ideas and important supporting details.
- Write only information that is useful and important to you. The information should be related to the ideas you are presenting in your report.
- Use your own words when you can. This will help you to think clearly about what you are reading and will help you use your own words in your report.
- When quoting directly from a source, use quotation marks to show that these notes are not in your own words.
- Use abbreviations and other writing short cuts to save time. The hints below show several short cuts.
- Abbreviate words, such as days of the week and state and country names.
- Use initials for names or key words after the first time you write them.
- Use short forms of words, such as *with* (w/). Make up your own short forms. The only rule is that you know what it means when you read your notes later.
- Use symbols for words, such as *equals* (=), *number* (#), and *and* (+).
- Make sure your notes are accurate.

Try It Out

A. Suppose you are writing a report about the American writer Anzia Yezierska. The report will answer the following questions: "What is Anzia Yezierska known for?" and "What difficulties did she overcome to become a writer?" Read the article about Anzia Yezierska on page 14. Then, on your own paper, take notes.

Anzia Yezierska was born in a village in Poland around 1880. Her family had almost no money. Around 1890, the family moved to the United States and settled in a poor section of New York City. Anzia could not go to school very often as a child. Her father did not believe that girls should have an education. From childhood on, Anzia had to work at whatever jobs she could, including selling paper bags on the street and working in laundries and sweatshops—small, overcrowded clothing factories.

Yet Anzia wanted to write. To get an education, she had to go to night school after a full day of work. Once she even got a much younger girl to lend her schoolbooks and teach her lessons from the books. The more Anzia learned, the more she wanted to write. She often wrote while she ate lunch at her job. When she did not have paper, she wrote on the back of her lunch bag. Most of her writings dealt with what it was like to grow up as an immigrant. Like her, the people in her stories faced prejudice because they were foreign. They also faced anger from their elders when they tried to give up the old ways of their homeland.

At first Anzia had trouble getting published. Then magazines began to print her stories. In the 1920s, she became a well-known writer. Her books include <u>Bread Givers</u> and <u>Red Ribbon on a White Horse</u>.

B. Underline the details in the article that answer the question "What difficulties did she overcome to become a writer?"

How To

Take Notes from More Than One Source

- When you already have information in your notes from an earlier source, don't record it again. Only note new facts or details.
- You might use index cards to take notes from several sources. You could put all the notes from one source on a separate card or set of cards.
- If two sources disagree on a fact, write down both versions of the fact. Consult your teacher to find how to state this fact in your report.

Try It Out

The notes on the following page were taken from a book about the ways glass affects light rays. The notes are followed by material from another source on the same subject. Take notes on the second source, noting only new facts or details.

Light rays = energy. Travel in straight lines. Clear flat glass is transparent—light rays pass straight through. Result: we see exactly what's on other side of glass.

Light is a form of energy that travels in straight lines. Light rays cannot pass through most objects. You see these objects because light rays bounce off the objects and toward your eyes. One material that light can pass through is glass. You see exactly what is on the other side of a piece of clear, flat glass because the light rays travel straight through the glass to the objects beyond. On the other hand, curved glass bends light rays so that they pass through at an angle. Glass that has at least one curved surface is called a lens. When you look through a lens, you do not see the exact image of the objects on the other side. The image you see might be curved, blurred, or a different size. Other clear materials, such as plastic and even water, can also act as lenses.

_____
_____
_____
_____
_____
_____

What Have I Learned?

What do you think are the three most important things to do when taking notes?

_____
_____
_____

LESSON 7

Developing an Outline from Notes

Putting notes into **outline** form helps organize information in a logical order. Think of an outline as a pattern or framework for the shape your report will take. In an outline, list the main ideas you will present, and follow them with details and other important information that support the main ideas.

Ask Yourself

Read the notes about pyramids. Then answer the questions that follow.

- Egyptian pyramids, probably the world's best-known pyramids
- Pyramids (Egypt) built between about 2700 B.C. and 1640 B.C.
- Pyramids also found in Western Hemisphere — Mexico, Central America, South America
- Pyramids in Mex., Cent. Amer., S. Amer. built by peoples such as the Maya, the Toltecs, and the Inca
- The Great Pyramid in Egypt about 450 feet high
- Pyramid of the Sun in Mexico about 206 feet high
- Western Hemisphere pyramids built from about A.D. 500 to A.D. 1500

1. Put a ✓ next to the two notes that seem to be the two most important ideas.

2. Underline the first main idea with a color.

3. With the same color, circle the supporting details for the first main idea.

4. Use another color to underline the second main idea.

16

5. With that same color, circle the supporting details for the second main idea.

You have just taken the first steps for organizing notes into an outline!

How To

Develop an Outline from Notes

- Review your report plan to identify your main ideas. Sort your notes according to main ideas and related information.
- It may help to rewrite notes on separate sheets of paper or on index cards. Or you might circle and underline in different colors.
- An outline is only a framework. As in your notes, use key words or phrases instead of complete sentences.
- Arrange the main ideas as **main headings,** using Roman numerals I., II., III., IV., and so on.
- Arrange subtopics that are related to (but less important than) each main idea as **subheadings** under each main heading, using capital letters A., B., C., and so on.
- Additional details about the subtopics should be arranged under each subheading using regular numerals 1., 2., 3., and so on. It is not necessary to always have details below each subtopic.
- Capitalize the first word of each main heading, subheading, and detail.

Shown below is a model outline.

> I. Alien ship comes to Earth November 23, 1992
>   A. Lands in Green Pines, New Jersey
>   1. Larger than a football stadium
>   2. Deafening roar
>   B. Aliens visible inside
>   1. Square heads, six eyes
>   2. No attempt to communicate with Earthlings
>
> II. Ship departs within three hours of landing
>   A. Ship emits rainbow trail as it soars upward
>   B. Aliens leave mysterious box behind
>   1. Strange sounds from within box
>   2. Scientists believe box may contain life form

Try It Out

A. Complete the outline below by using the following notes.

Uses of horses—work and recreation
—Recreation: horses in sports, including riding and sports such as polo
—Work: many horses used for transportation carry loads and people
—Work: horses used for transportation also pull wagons or carts
—Recreation: horses used for entertainment, including circuses
—Work: Horses do farm and ranch work
—Work: In some parts of the world, horses still pull plows
—Work: Many ranch workers round up cattle on horseback
—Recreation: Horses used for entertainment in movies, especially Westerns

Topic: Horses in the World Today

I. Horses used for work

   A. _____

      1. _____

      2. _____

   B. Farm and ranch work

      1. _____

      2. _____

II. Horses used in recreation

   A. Sports

      1. _____

      2. _____

   B. _____

      1. _____

      2. _____

B. Use the notes below to make an outline with two main heads. The notes are for a report on Jim Thorpe, a Native American athlete. Thorpe excelled in two kinds of sports—Olympic sports and professional sports.

Topic: Jim Thorpe's Sports Achievements
- Thorpe was in the Olympics
- Won two Olympic medals in Stockholm, Sweden, in 1912
- Won gold medal in Stockholm for the decathlon—a sport that includes long jump, running, discus throw, etc.
- Thorpe was also a professional athlete
- Thorpe played pro baseball for the New York Giants and the Cincinnati Reds
- Played professional football between 1915 and 1929
- In Stockholm Olympics, Thorpe also won gold medal for pentathlon

What Have I Learned?

How will writing an outline help you decide what to write in each paragraph of a report? Use your own paper to write your answer.

LESSON 8
Writing a First Draft

When you have arranged all your information in outline form, write a **first draft**. A first draft is like a rehearsal for the final report. It does not have to be perfect.

Ask Yourself

The partial outline below was used to begin a first draft of the report about Léopold Senghor of Senegal. Read the outline and first draft, and then follow the directions.

I. Senghor was one of Africa's leading statesmen through a long career
   A. While Senegal was a French colony
      1. Represented Senegal in French National Assembly (similar to U.S. Congress)
      2. In 1948, founded a political party supporting independence
   B. After Senegal became independent in 1960
      1. Senghor became Senegal's first president
      2. Other European countries had colonies
      3. Served as president until 1981

> Léopold Senghor had a long career as one of Africa's leading statesmen. In 1948, Senghor founded a political party that supported independence. When Senegal became independent in 1960, Senghor became its first president. Other European countries that had African colonies at that time included Britain, Portugal, and Belgium. While Senegal was a French colony, Senghor represented Senegal in France's congress, the French National Assembly. Senghor served as Senegal's president until 1981.

1. Circle the sentence that contains the main idea from the outline.

2. Underline the sentences that contain the subtopics from the outline.

3. Draw a line through the detail that does not belong in this paragraph.

How do you think a teacher would have marked this paragraph if it had been turned in as a final draft instead of used as a first draft?

How To

Write a First Draft

- Many reports have an introductory paragraph, two or more central paragraphs, and a concluding paragraph.
- The first paragraph should introduce your topic or present it in a general way.
- Each of the central paragraphs should contain a main idea. Each main idea is based on a main head from your outline. The details supporting the main idea come from the topics and details in your outline.
- The last, or concluding, paragraph presents statements that pull your ideas together and form a conclusion.
- Remember to use your own words. Never copy sentences from research sources, unless you use them as direct quotations.

Try It Out

Read the outline that starts below. Use the outline to write a first draft of a report about the Great Wall of China. The introductory paragraph, taken from the first section of the outline, has already been written for you. It is on page 23. Use the lines provided to complete the first draft.

Outline

I. Great Wall of China is world's longest structure
    A. Other famous structures not nearly as long
        1. California's Golden Gate Bridge—4,200 feet
        2. Egypt's Suez Canal—100 miles
    B. Great Wall longest structure <u>ever</u> built
        1. 4,000 miles long
        2. Crosses northern China
        3. Built all by hand, at a time before machines

II. Wall's size and appearance
    A. Made of stone, bricks, and earth
        1. Stone and bricks in eastern China
        2. Mostly packed earth in western China, where stone and brickmaking materials scarce

   B. 4,000-mile wall is wide enough to walk on
       1. 15 feet wide at top
       2. Used as a road by soldiers and workers who were building it
       3. Lookout towers (every 100 to 200 yards in wall) had flat tops so people could stand or walk there

III. Built from about 400 B.C. to A.D. 1600
   A. At first, only separate sections built
   B. In 200 B.C. Emperor Shi Huangdi planned a continuous wall
       1. He had many of the separate sections connected
       2. Purpose: to protect China from outside attackers
   C. Work continued for hundreds of years
       1. Wall largely completed by A.D. 200
       2. Parts of wall repaired or rebuilt from A.D. 1300 to A.D. 1600

IV. Today, wall is a tourist attraction
   A. Many visitors from other countries take walks along the wall
   B. World leaders, including U.S. and Russian presidents, visit wall

First Draft

The Great Wall of China

The world's longest structure is not the 4,200-foot-long Golden Gate Bridge or even the 100-mile-long Suez Canal. It is the Great Wall of China. This huge wall is over 4,000 miles long and is the longest structure ever built. More amazing is that it was built at a time when there were no machines to help the people who built it. Workers built it all by hand.

What Have I Learned?

Which was the hardest paragraph of your report to write? Why?

LESSON 9

Revising and Proofreading for a Final Report

Your first draft contains the information you will present in your final report. After you write the draft, it should be revised to improve the wording. This is also the time to **proofread** your draft, correcting errors in spelling, capitalization, and punctuation. When you complete your revisions and corrections, make a final copy, using the format your teacher directs you to use.

Ask Yourself

Read the first draft below, using the checklist that follows to examine it. Write yes or no before each item to show whether you found each mistake.

> Today many rock stars are known for their glittery on-stage costumes? They are not the first performers to wear wonderful costumes, however. Dancers from countries such as Mexico, russia, Bolivia Thailand, and India have been dressing to amaze for thousands of years. Some of these countries share a border with each other. Dancers have worn such things as gold, gems, silk, and towering headdresses of feathers as part of their dance costumes. Dancers have worn fancy masks, too.

_____ 1. Are there too many sentences in a row that begin with the same word?

_____ 2. Are there any details that do not belong in the paragraph?

_____ 3. Are there any sentences that are not complete?

24

_____ **4.** Are any sentences missing an end punctuation mark?

_____ **5.** Do any sentences end with the wrong punctuation mark?

_____ **6.** Are there any errors in capitalization?

_____ **7.** Are there any places where a comma needs to be added?

_____ **8.** Are any words misspelled?

Did you write <u>yes</u> for six items, 1, 2, 5, 6, and 7? If so, you were correct.

How To

Revise and Proofread for a Final Report

- Reread your work carefully. Be sure you have followed the rules listed below.
- Stick to your topic. Do not include details that do not belong.
- Make sure your main ideas are clear. All sentences should give additional details or facts about your main ideas.
- Break up any of your paragraphs into two paragraphs if necessary.
- Write complete sentences. Make sure all your sentences start with capital letters and end with appropriate punctuation.
- Spell all words correctly. Use a dictionary if you are unsure of spellings.
- Use the proofreader's marks shown on the next page.
- If too many sentences in a row start with the same word, such as *he* or *the*, rearrange the words in some of your sentences.
- If all of your sentences are short and choppy, think about connecting some pairs of sentences with a word, such as *and* or *but*.
- Start some sentences with transition words so readers can follow your ideas better. Use these words carefully though, because they can change the meaning of your sentence. Following is a list of transition words or phrases:

| first | next | therefore | as a result | because of |
| however | finally | for example | in addition | in the same way |

Try It Out

A. Review the first draft in *Ask Yourself*. Use the proofreader's marks to correct the mistakes you found. Use the **How To** tips to help you decide whether any sentences need to be rewritten. Then write the corrected paragraph on another sheet of paper.

Proofreader's Marks

Mark	Meaning
~~but~~ e	Cross this word out.
b^r^ave	Add this letter or word.
~~four~~ for	Change this word.
me (underlined)	Make this a capital letter.
The (slash through T)	Make this a lower-case letter.
¶ He is	Begin a new paragraph.
end ⊙	Add a period.
happy‸but	Add a comma.
was (transpose mark)	Change this word order.

B. Read the first draft of a report. Then follow the directions to mark your corrections. Make corrections on the draft.

Small-size models against a scenery backround are a very useful kind of special effect. Small models are easier to film than full-size objects because they are easier to move around in front of a camera. They are cheaper because less material is needed to make them They can be filmed in a little room instead of on a large, expensive sound stage. Any film that uses special effects can make use of small models, but some types of films depend on these models. one example of a kind of film that uses small-size models in many places during filming is space action movies like <u>Star Wars</u>. The "giant" space ships can often be no bigger than a toy car. James Earl Jones played the voice of one <u>Star Wars</u> character. Monstir movies are another kind of film that depends on models. They often use models small for the monster. In <u>King Kong</u>, the huge ape used in many scenes was really only about two feet tall.

26

1. Use the paragraph symbol to divide this paragraph into two paragraphs.

2. Find the two words that are misspelled. Use a dictionary if you need to. In the report, use the mark for crossing out, and write the correct spelling.

3. Use the capital and lower-case letter marks to show needed corrections.

4. Add any missing end punctuation to the draft.

5. In the next to the last sentence, two words are out of order. Use the ⁀ mark to fix the word order.

6. Find the detail that does not belong in this paragraph. Use the mark for crossing out to remove it.

7. If appropriate, insert a transition word or phrase to start a sentence. Use the ∧ mark to show that you are adding that word or phrase.

8. There are too many sentences in a row that start with the same word. Think of a way to reword them. You may change word order, add or substitute words, or join two sentences to make one longer sentence. Write your corrected sentences here.

_____
_____
_____
_____
_____
_____
_____

What Have I Learned?

Look at several reports and other written assignments you have written recently. Suppose you could revise them to hand in again. Which revising or proofreading hints do you need the most to work on in these assignments?

_____
_____
_____
_____

LESSON 10 — Preparing a Bibliography

You are often asked to include at the end of a research report an alphabetical list of reference sources from which you gathered your information. This is called a **bibliography**. Record the details for your bibliography at the same time you take research notes. This saves you time and effort later.

Ask Yourself

Suppose a student wrote a report about robots. Use his bibliography shown below to answer the questions.

Baldwin, Margaret, and Peck, Gary. Robots and Robotics. New York: Franklin Watts, Inc., 1984.

Macauley, David. The Way Things Work. Boston: Houghton Mifflin Co., 1988.

Moffett, Mark W. "Dance of the Electronic Bee." National Geographic, January 1990, pp. 134–140.

The World Book Encyclopedia. 1989 ed. "Robot."

1. What encyclopedia did the student consult when he wrote his report?
   _____

2. What magazine did he use?
   _____

3. What two books did he use?
   _____
   _____

4. What is the most recently published reference source he used?
   _____

5. Which of the student's sources has two authors?
   _____

As you see, you can learn a lot about a report from the bibliography. Do you think the writer of the report on robots used a good variety of sources?

How To

Prepare a Bibliography

- When taking notes, record the name of the source, the title of the newspaper or magazine article, page numbers of articles, author(s), publication or edition date, book publisher and city.
- Decide whether each source is a nonfiction book, an encyclopedia article, or a newspaper or magazine article. Use the bibliography from *Ask Yourself* to see how each source should be listed. An entry for a newspaper article should be written like the entry for a magazine article.
- Ask your teacher how to list unusual information sources, such as videotapes.
- List your entries in alphabetical order. For an encyclopedia article, use the first main word (not *The*) of the encyclopedia's title. Use the author's last name for all other types of sources. If there are two authors, use the name of the first author mentioned in the source to alphabetize.
- If a magazine article gives a list of authors, list the first name and then the words *et al.*, which mean "and others." Example: *Vance, Susan, et al.*

Try It Out

Write a bibliography that shows the following four information sources. List your entries in the correct format and in alphabetical order.

<u>Abraham Lincoln</u> by Lee Morgan and Pietro Cattaneo, Silver Burdett Press, Englewood Cliffs, New Jersey: 1990.
Encyclopedia article, <u>The New Book of Knowledge</u>, 1990. "Abraham Lincoln."
Magazine article from <u>Newsweek</u> by Jerry Adler and other authors, "Revisiting the Civil War." Oct. 8, 1990, pp. 58--64.
<u>Lincoln: A Photobiography</u> by Russell Freedman, 1987, Clarion Books, New York.

_____
_____
_____
_____
_____

What Have I Learned?

On your own paper, describe the kind of information a bibliography contains.

REVIEW: Planning a Report

LESSONS 1–3

Reviewing What You Learned

Write the answer to each question.

1. What kind of information sources do you need to use for a research report?
   _____

2. What information supports the main ideas in a report?
   _____

3. Why do you need to narrow a topic?
   _____

4. What can you write down ahead of time to help plan your research?
   _____

Using What You Know

Choose two topics from this list: a famous person you are interested in; a specific machine, tool, or invention; a specific animal; a hobby you know about. Write these two topics in the top sections of the chart. Then complete the chart.

	Topic One	Topic Two
Write a broad topic.	_____	_____
Narrow the topic.	_____	_____
Write two questions you want your report to answer about that topic.	1. _____ 2. _____	1. _____ 2. _____

REVIEW

Gathering and Organizing Information

LESSONS 4–7

Reviewing What You Learned

Write true or false beside each sentence.

_____ **1.** An encyclopedia would be the best place to find information about an event that happened last week.

_____ **2.** One way to find information quickly is to scan a page looking for headings and other key words.

_____ **3.** You need to write an outline of your report before you can start taking notes from an information source.

_____ **4.** In an outline, the most important ideas are arranged as main heads.

Using What You Know

A report on the Ashanti of Africa will answer the questions "Who and where are the Ashanti?" and "What is the history of the Ashanti?" Use the notes below to make an outline that has two main sections. Use your own paper.

- Ashanti—ethnic group in Ghana in Africa
- Ashanti people part of kingdom, then empire, then country of Ghana
- Ashanti are Ghana's largest ethnic group
- today, have more power in Ghana than any other ethnic group
- kingdom began in late 1600s
- empire: early 1800s, parts of present-day Ghana, Togo, and Ivory Coast
- empire ended in late 1800s in fight with Britain over trade routes
- then Ashanti became colony of British empire
- Ashanti people gained independence in 1957 as part of country of Ghana
- kingdom: in 1600s, Ashanti people united by Osei Tutu, Ashanti leader
- Osei Tutu became first king
- Ashanti population about 1½ million

REVIEW — Writing a Report

LESSONS 8–10

Reviewing What You Learned

Write the word or phrase that best completes each sentence.

1. When you write a report, each paragraph will contain a _____ _____ and subtopics from one section of your outline.

2. Many reports contain an introductory paragraph, two central paragraphs, and a _____.

3. After writing your first draft, proofread it to find errors in spelling, _____, and punctuation.

4. A bibliography is a list of the reference sources used in a report. The entries are shown in _____ order.

Using What You Know

The paragraphs below are part of a first draft. Read the paragraphs through once. Then revise and proofread them. Write proofreader's marks on this draft. Write your final draft on your own paper.

> Jacqueline Cochran was one of the most famous woman pilots in American history. she began flying in 1932. In 1934, she was the only woman to fly in an air race from London, England, to Melbourne, australia. In 1935, she was the first woman to fly in another air race, the Bendix Transcontinental Air Race?
>
> Jacqueline cochran is best known for her deeds during World War II. Before the U.S. entered the war, Cochran trained women in England to fly transport planes These plains would carry supplies to soldiers on the battlefield. There were no airplanes during the Civil War, just trains. When the U.S. joined the war, Cochran returned home to train American women as pilots. She organized and directed the WASPS—the Women's Airforce Service Pilots. After World War II, Jacqueline Cochran was the first woman to Receive the Distinguished Service Medal.

32